This Book Belongs to

_____

_____

_____

Certificate
of
Completion

Aa Bb Cc Dd Ee

Ff Gg Hh Ii Jj Kk

Ll Mm Nn Oo Pp

Qq Rr Ss Tt Uu Vv

Ww Xx Yy Zz

0 1 2 3 4 5

6 7 8 9 10

 # Basic Strokes

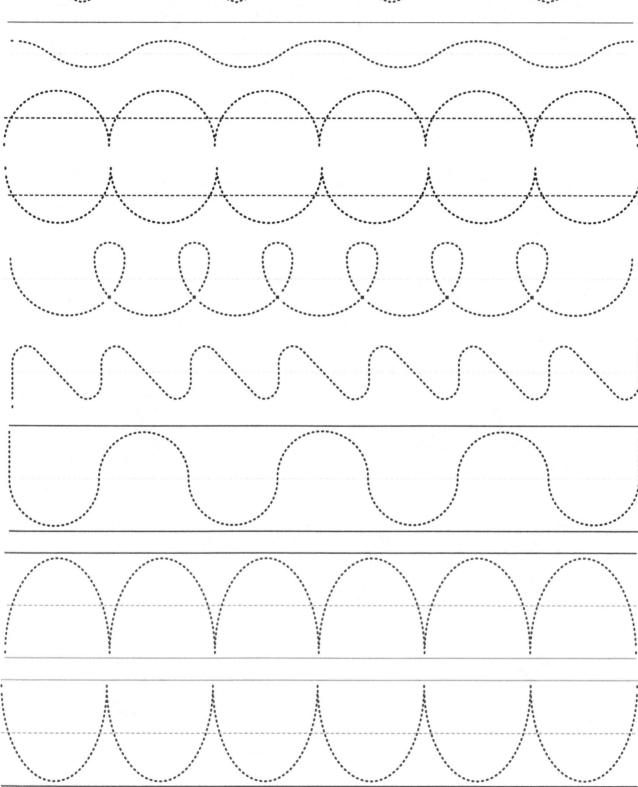

Basic Strokes

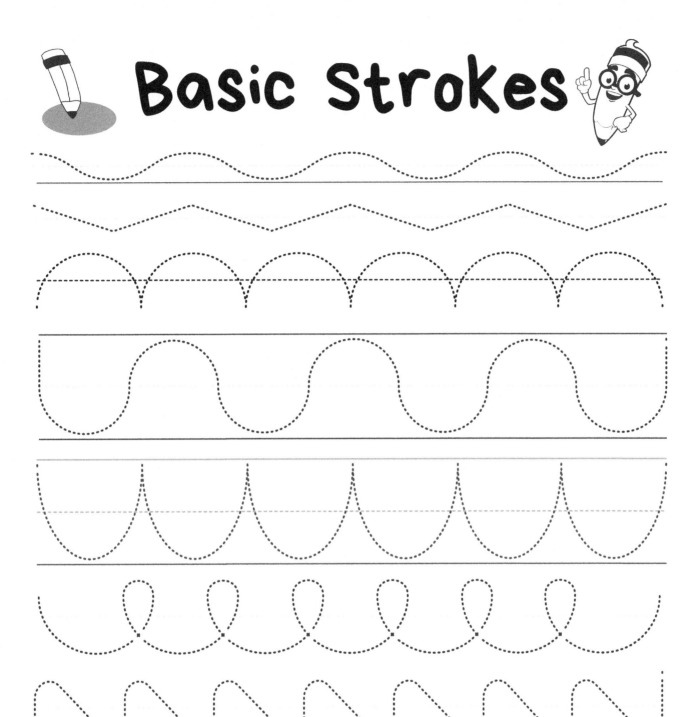

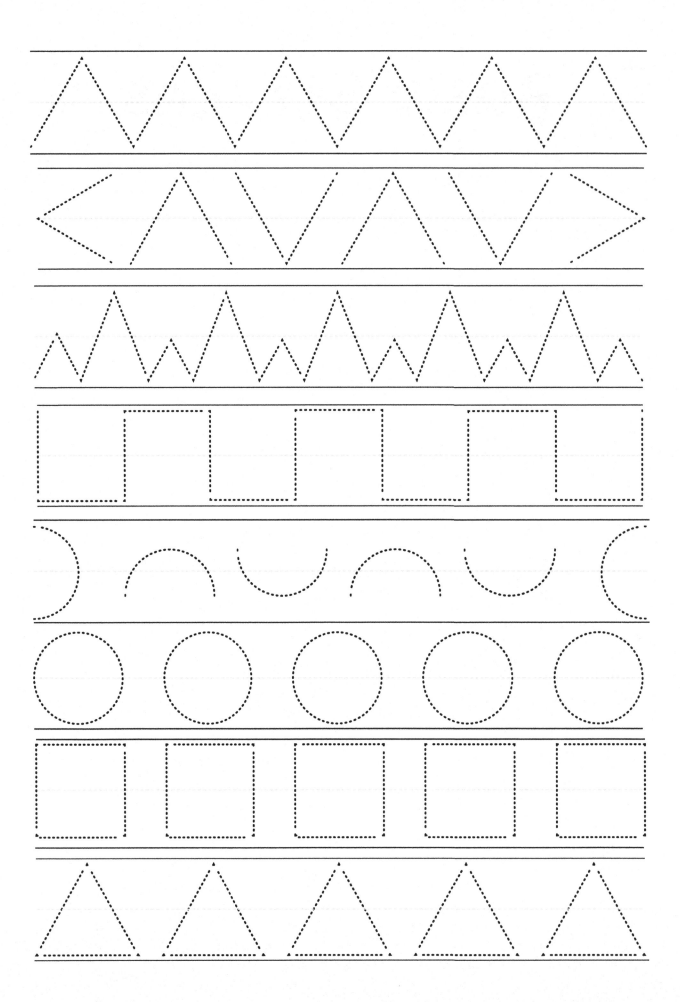

Basic Strokes

Trace the stoke lines & practice

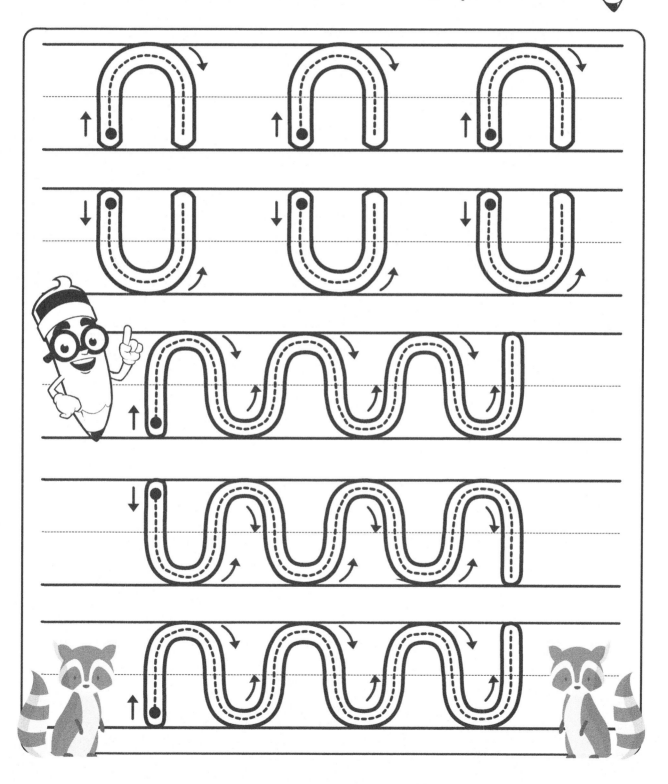

Basic Strokes

Trace the stoke lines & practice

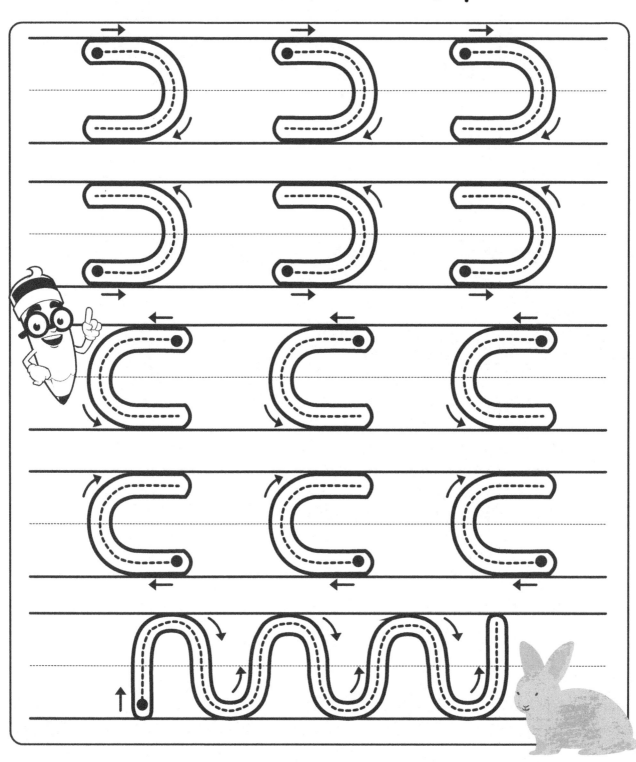

Basic Strokes

Trace The Lines & Practice

Basic Strokes

Trace The Lines & Practice

Letter Tracing
Upper Case

✏️ Trace the letter and color the picture.

Airplane

✏️ Trace the letter "A" and practice writing.

A A A A A A A A A

Letter Tracing
Lower Case

Trace the letter and color the picture.

ant

Trace the letter "a" and practice writing.

a

Letter Tracing
Upper Case

✏️ Trace the letter and color the picture.

Bee

✏️ Trace the letter "B" and practice writing.

Letter Tracing
Lower Case

Trace the letter and color the picture.

ball

Trace the letter "b" and practice writing.

b b b b b b b b b

Letter Tracing
Upper Case

Trace the letter and color the picture.

Clown

C

Trace the letter "C" and practice writing.

C   C   C   C   C   C   C

Letter Tracing
Lower Case

Trace the letter and color the picture.

cap

Trace the letter "c" and practice writing.

c c c c c c c c

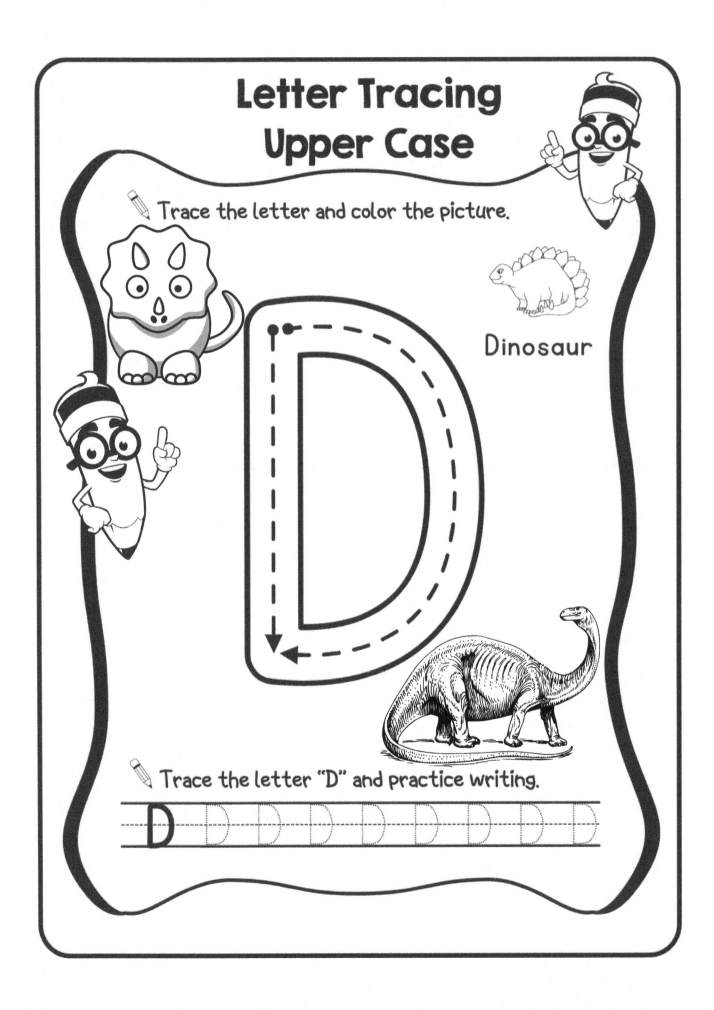

Letter Tracing
Upper Case

Trace the letter and color the picture.

Dinosaur

D

Trace the letter "D" and practice writing.

D D D D D D D D D D

Letter Tracing
Lower Case

Trace the letter and color the picture.

duck

Trace the letter "d" and practice writing.

d d d d d d d d d

Letter Tracing
Upper Case

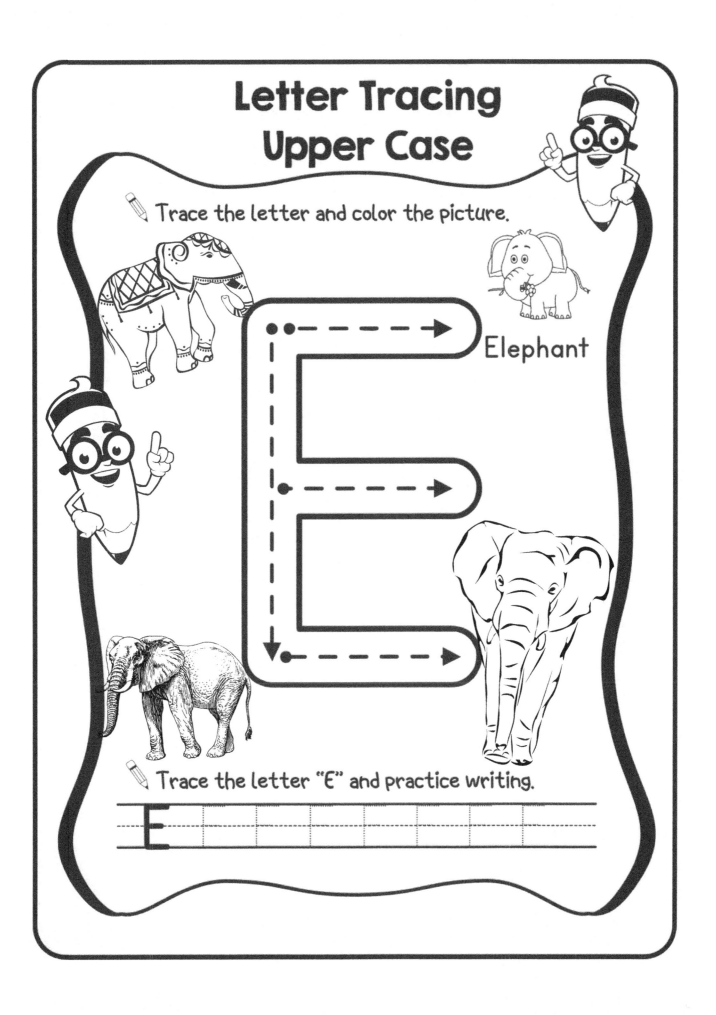

Trace the letter and color the picture.

Elephant

Trace the letter "E" and practice writing.

Letter Tracing
Lower Case

Trace the letter and color the picture.

eggplant

Trace the letter "e" and practice writing.

e e e e e e e e e

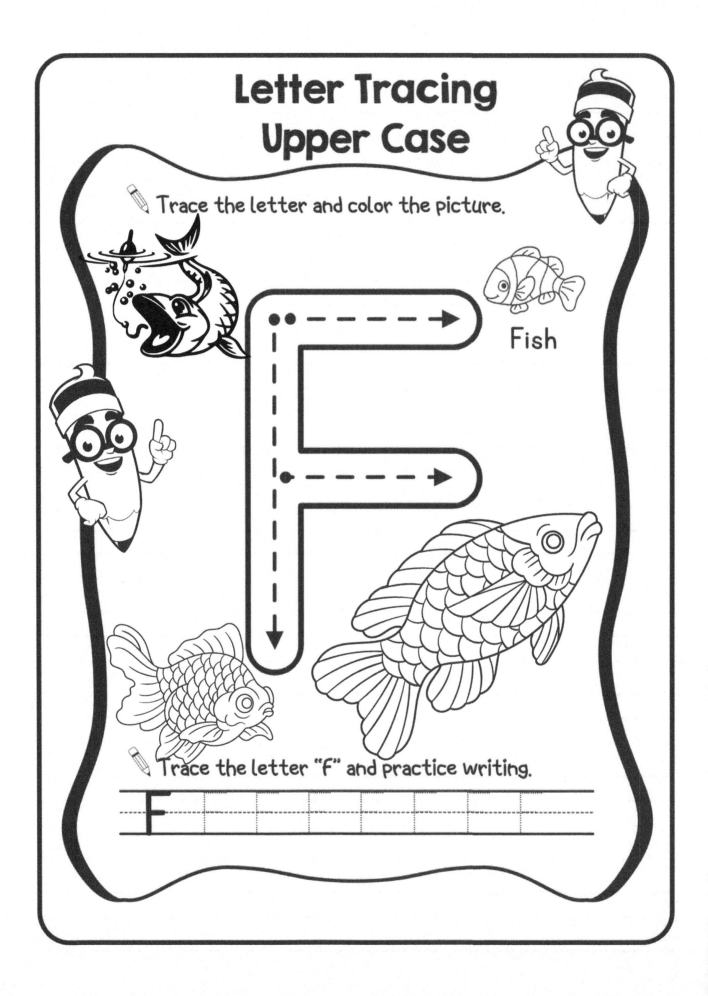

Letter Tracing
Upper Case

Trace the letter and color the picture.

Fish

Trace the letter "f" and practice writing.

F

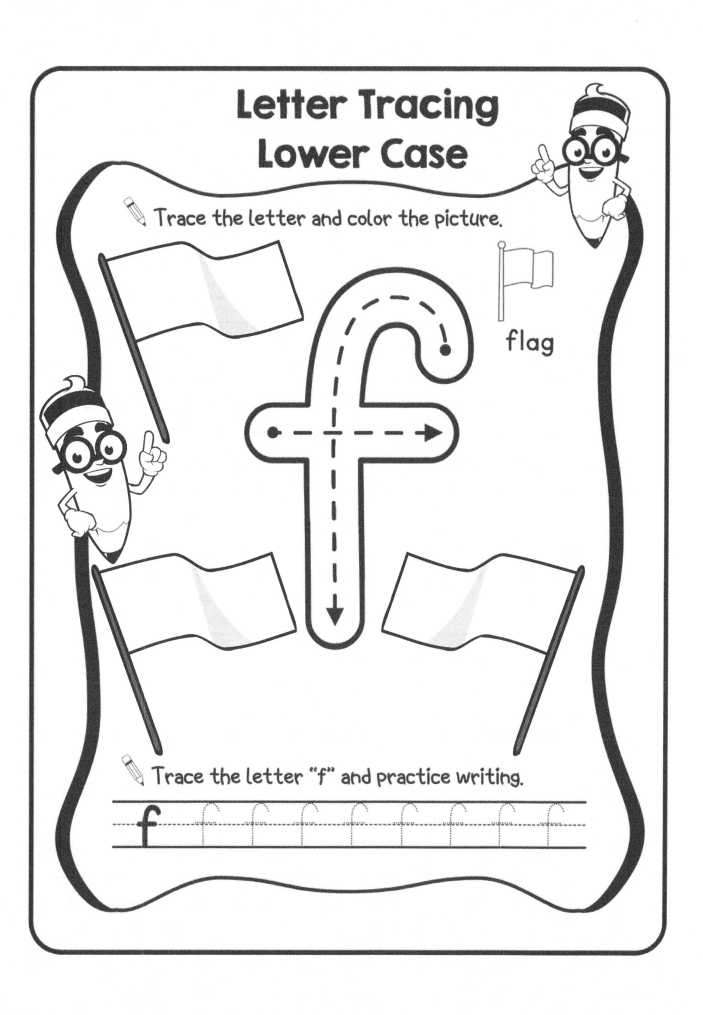

Letter Tracing
Lower Case

Trace the letter and color the picture.

flag

Trace the letter "f" and practice writing.

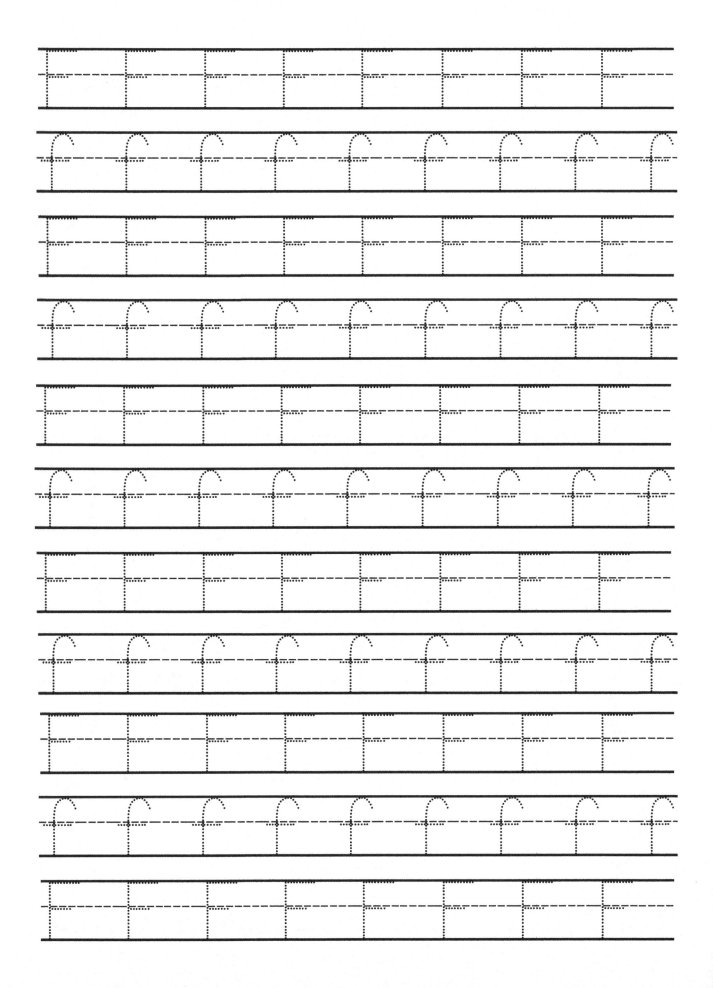

Letter Tracing
Upper Case

Trace the letter and color the picture.

Giraffe

G

Trace the letter "G" and practice writing.

G G G G G G G G

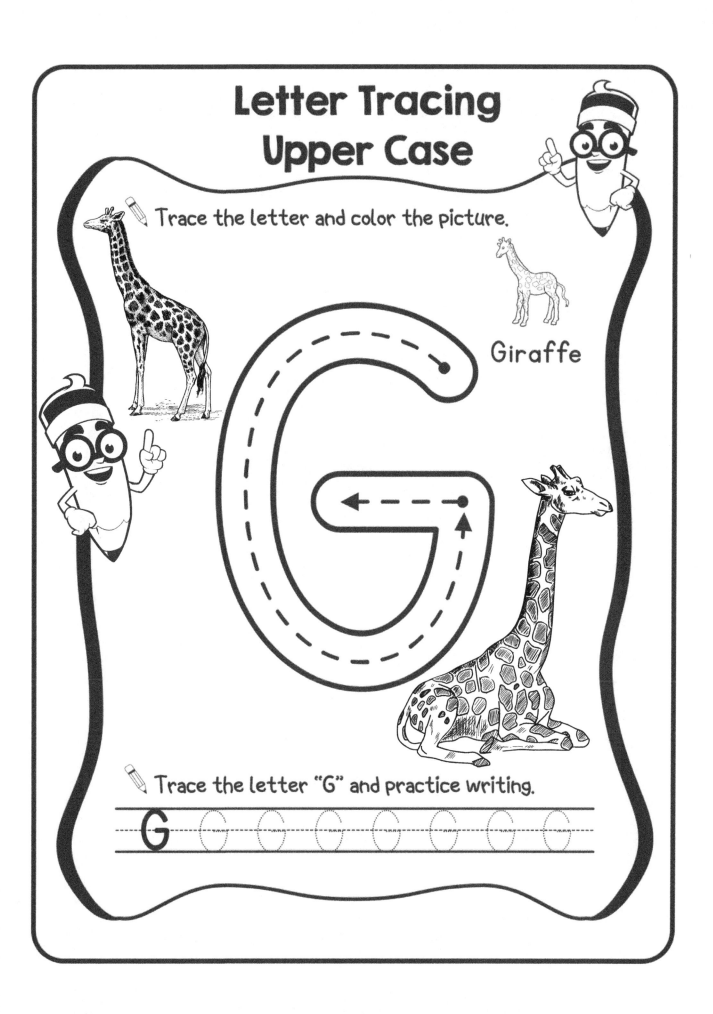

Letter Tracing
Lower Case

✏️ Trace the letter and color the picture.

gift

✏️ Trace the letter "g" and practice writing.

g g g g g g g g g

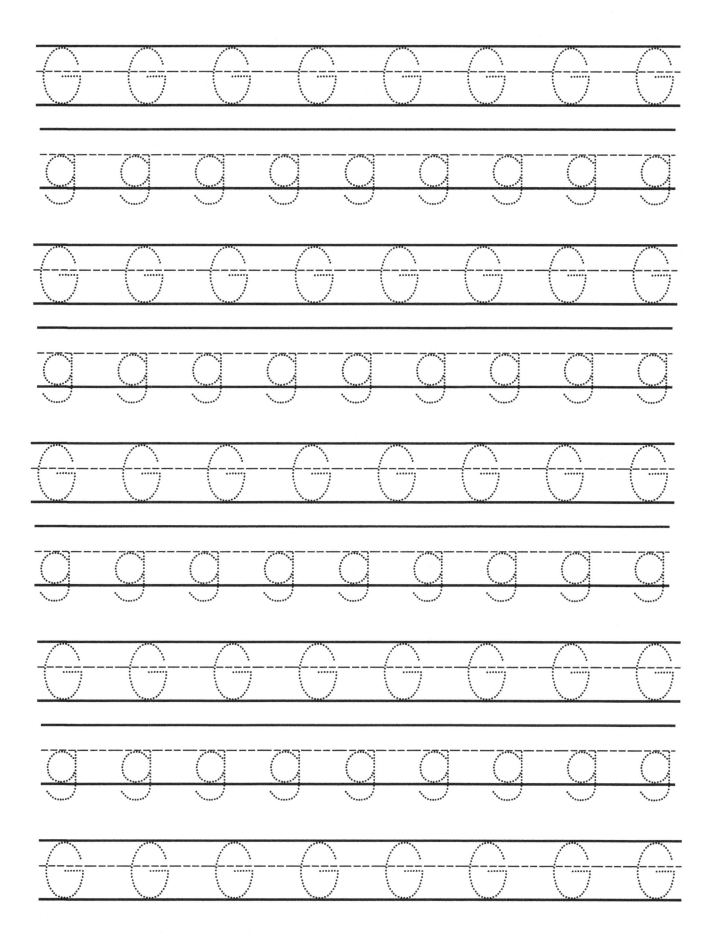

Letter Tracing
Upper Case

✏️ Trace the letter and color the picture.

House

H

✏️ Trace the letter "H" and practice writing.

H

Letter Tracing
Lower Case

Trace the letter and color the picture.

hat

Trace the letter "h" and practice writing.

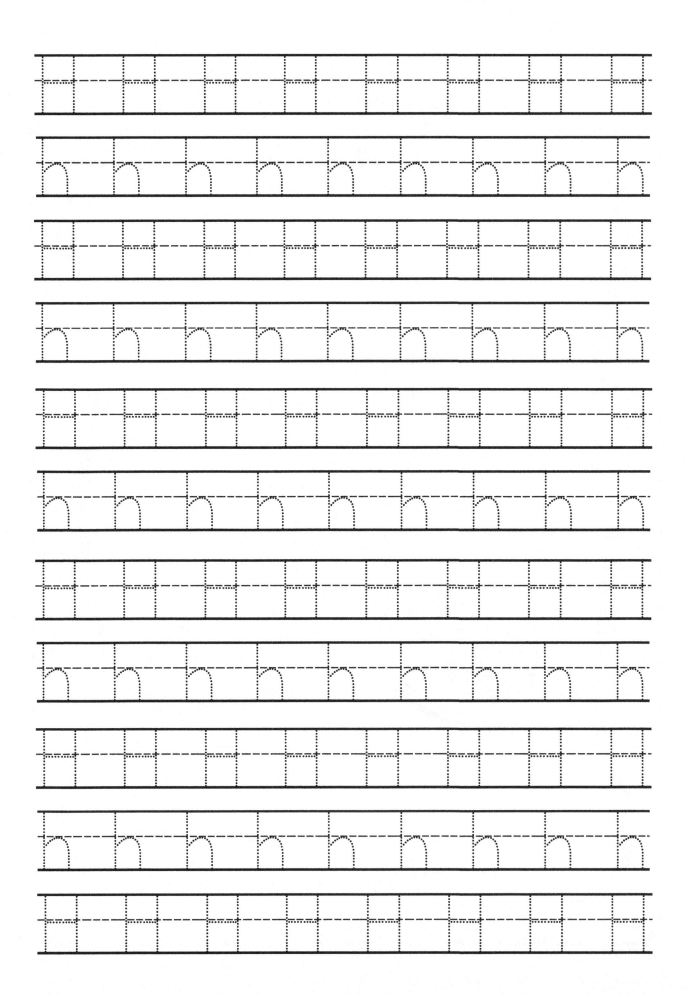

Letter Tracing
Upper Case

Trace the letter and color the picture.

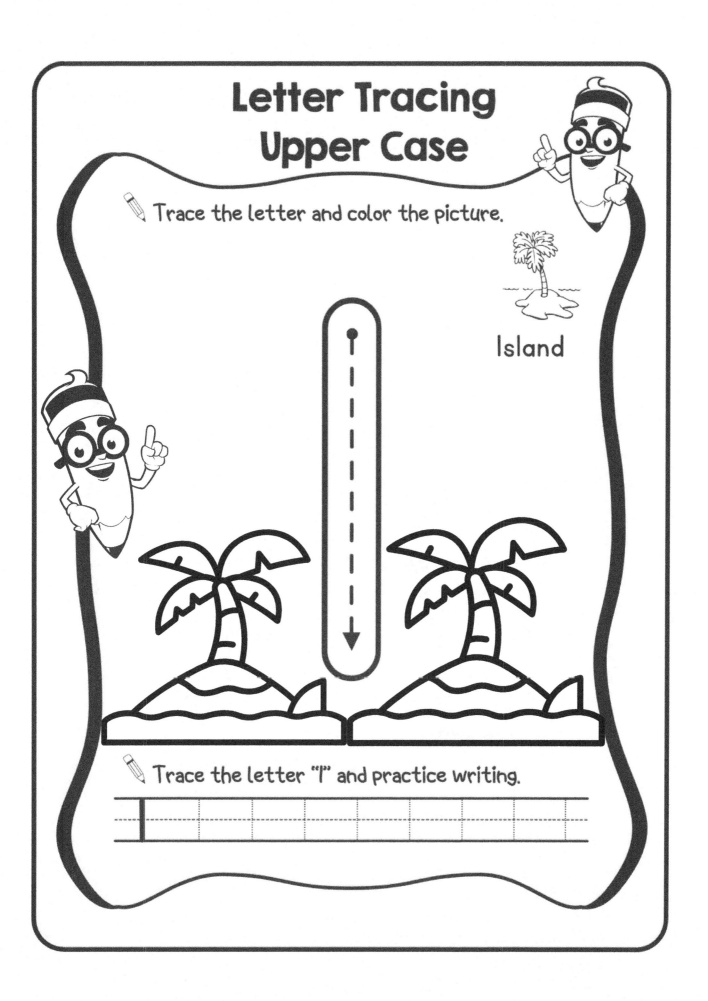

Island

Trace the letter "I" and practice writing.

Letter Tracing
Lower Case

✏️ Trace the letter and color the picture.

icecream

✏️ Trace the letter " i " and practice writing.

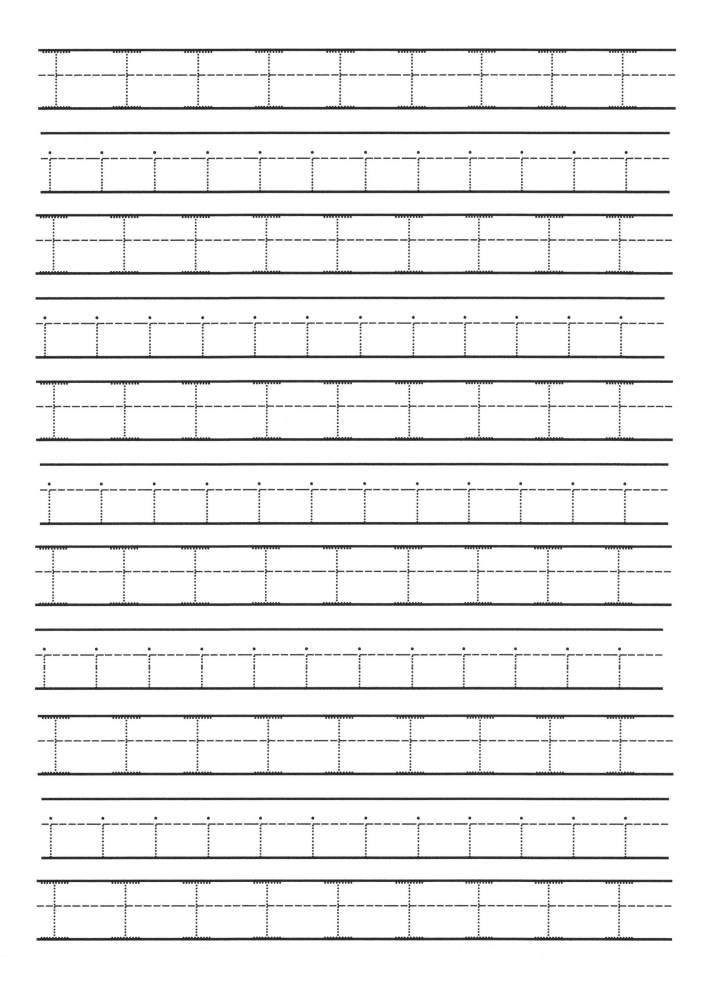

Letter Tracing
Upper Case

Trace the letter and color the picture.

Jacket

Trace the letter "J" and practice writing.

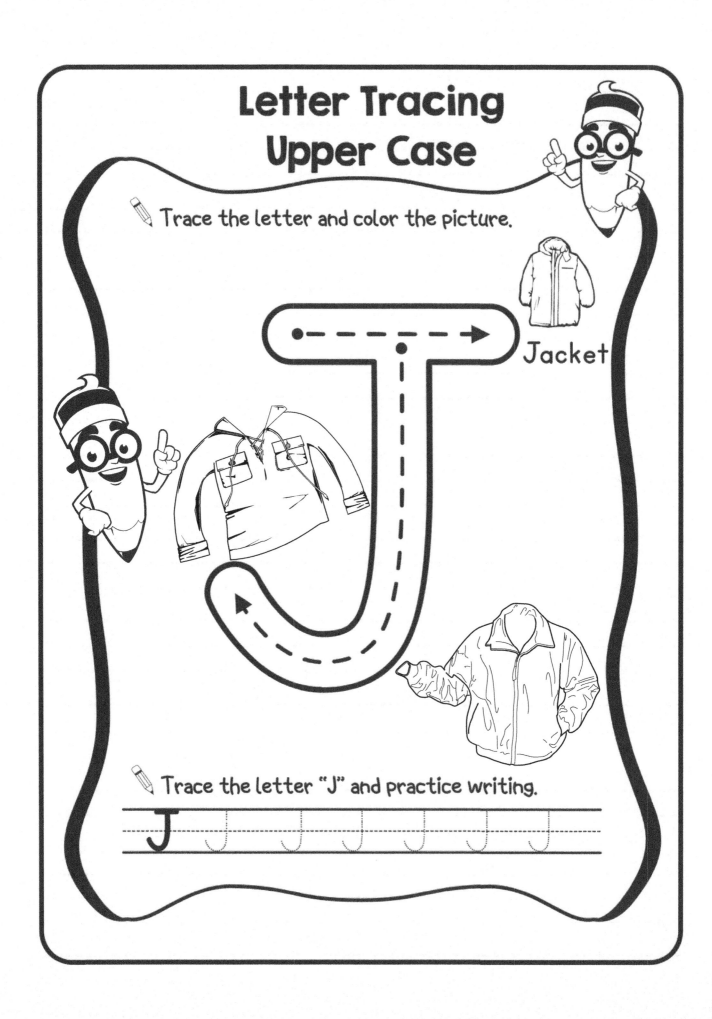

Letter Tracing
Lower Case

Trace the letter and color the picture.

jelly

Trace the letter "j" and practice writing.

j j j j j j j j j j j j j j j j

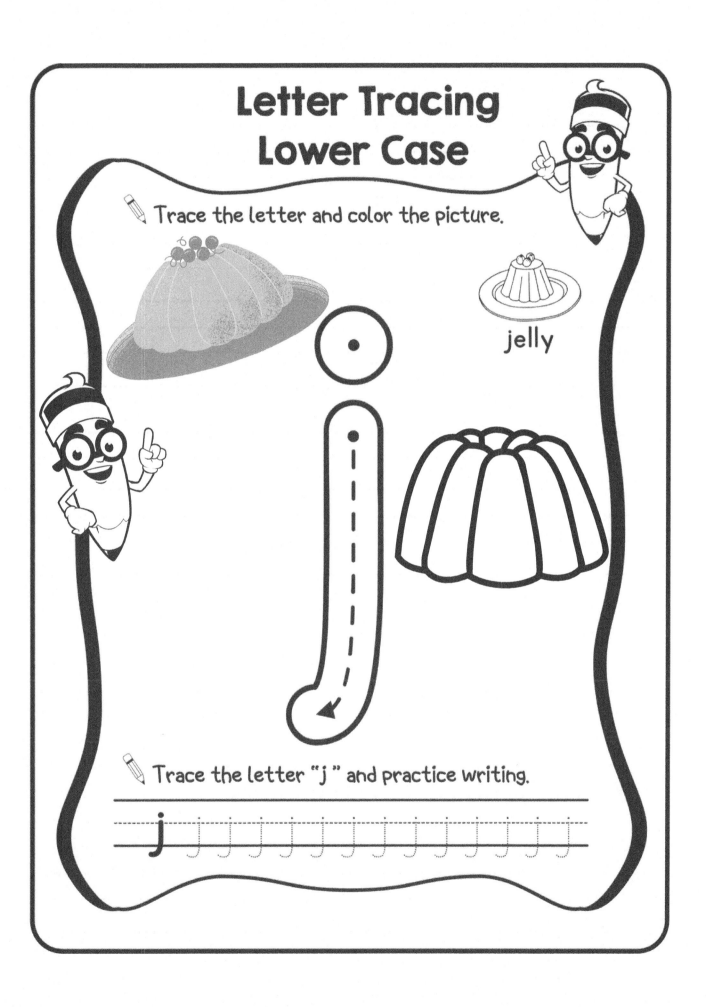

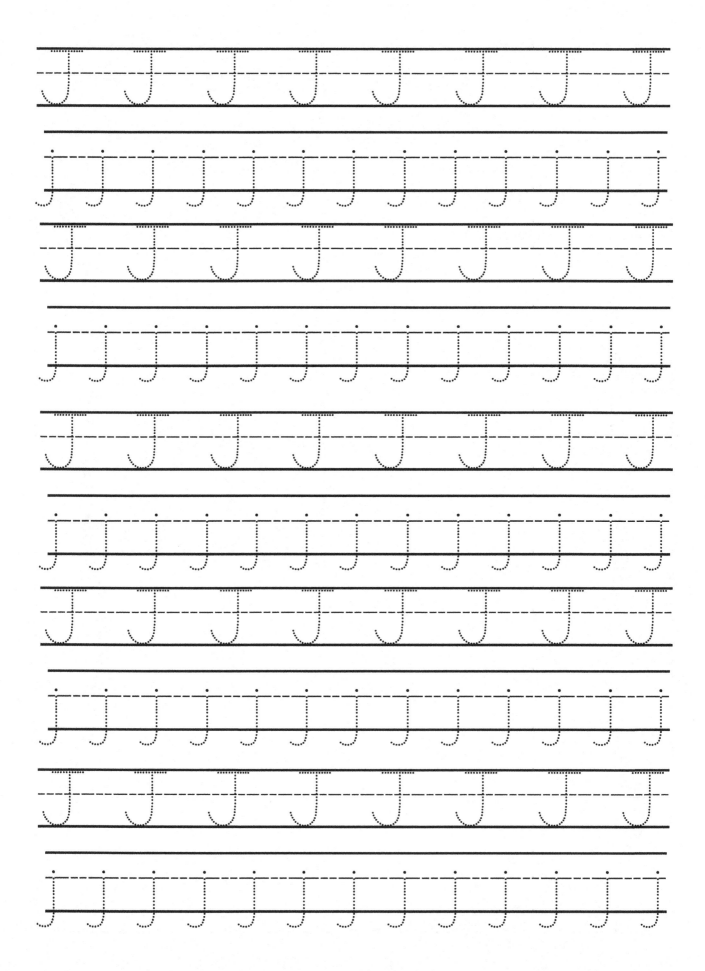

Letter Tracing
Upper Case

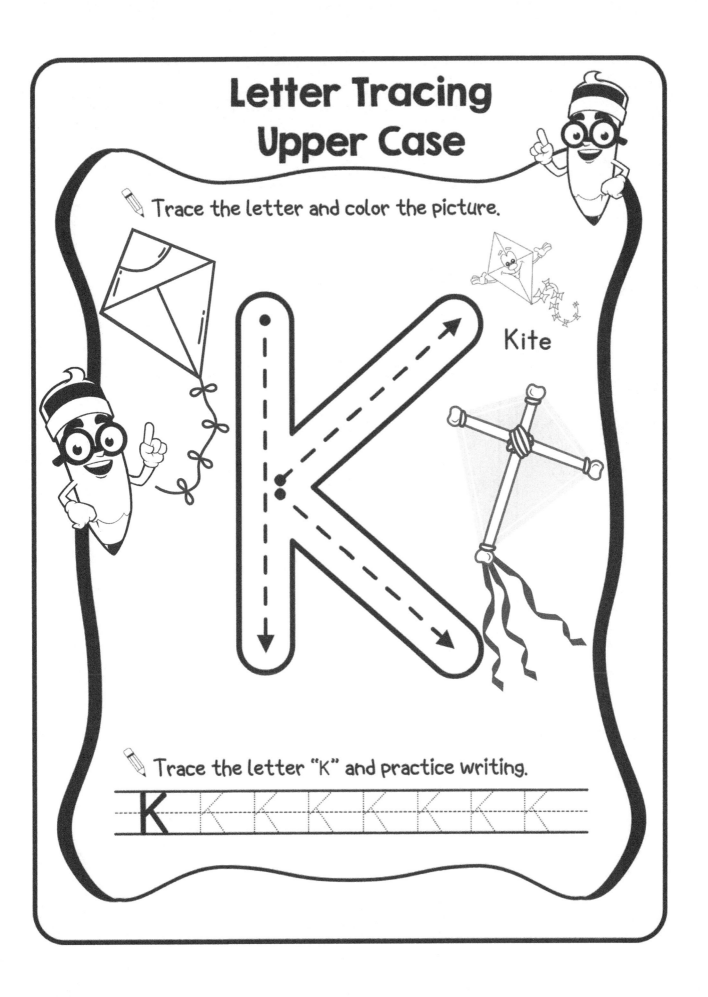

Trace the letter and color the picture.

Kite

Trace the letter "K" and practice writing.

K K K K K K K

Letter Tracing
Lower Case

✏️ Trace the letter and color the picture.

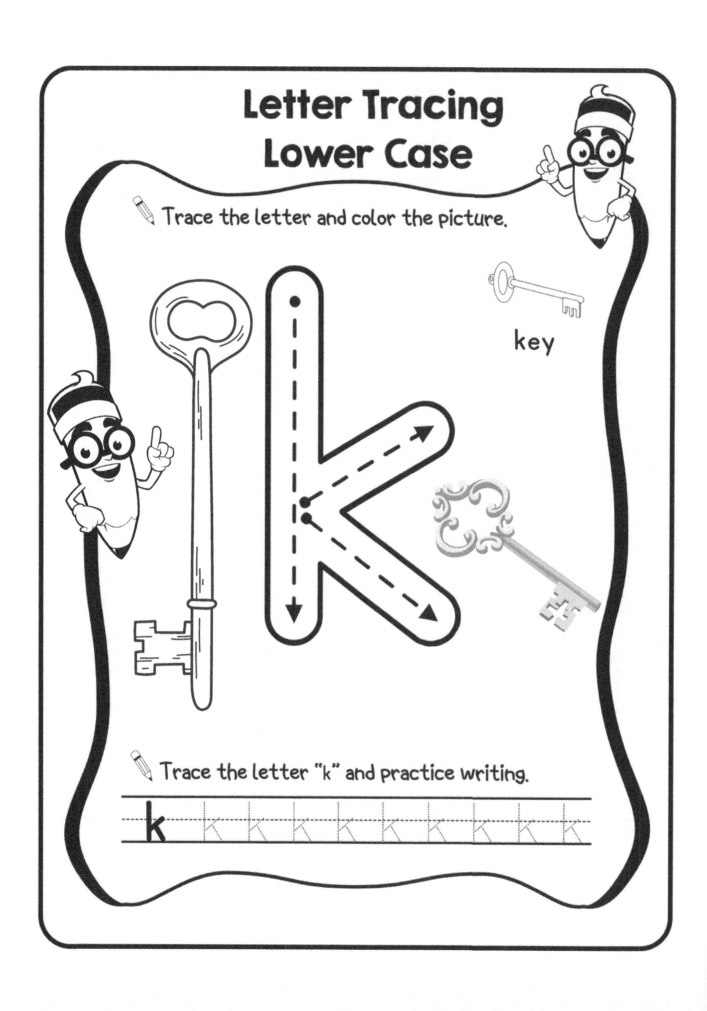

key

✏️ Trace the letter "k" and practice writing.

k k k k k k k k k

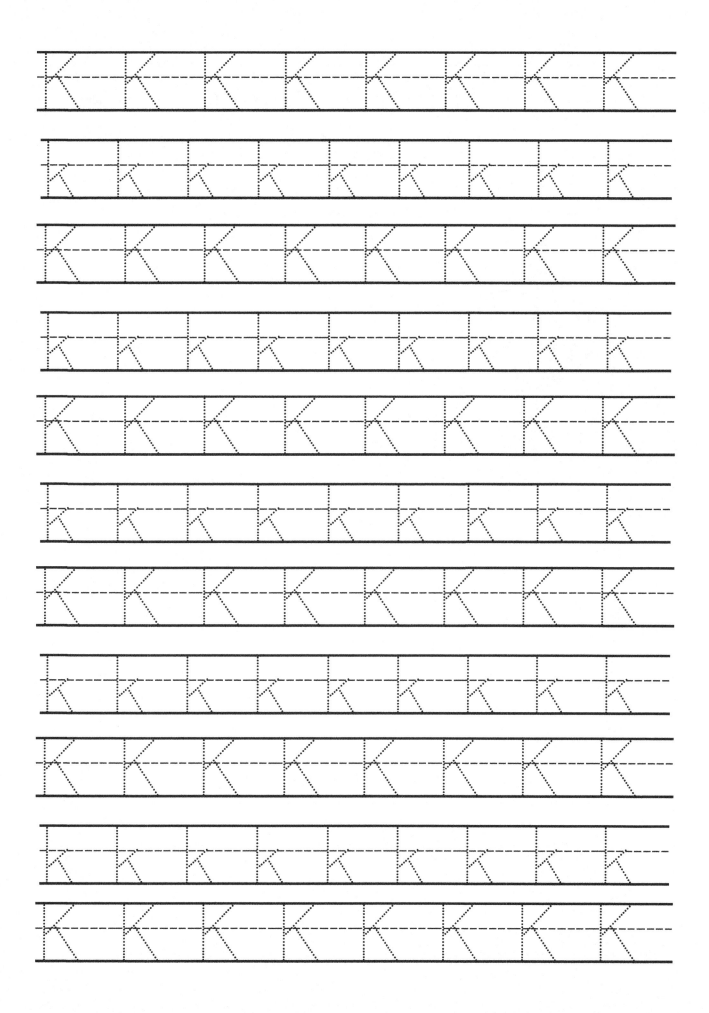

Letter Tracing
Upper Case

Trace the letter and color the picture.

Lantern

Trace the letter "L" and practice writing.

Letter Tracing
Lower Case

Trace the letter and color the picture.

leaf

Trace the letter "l" and practice writing.

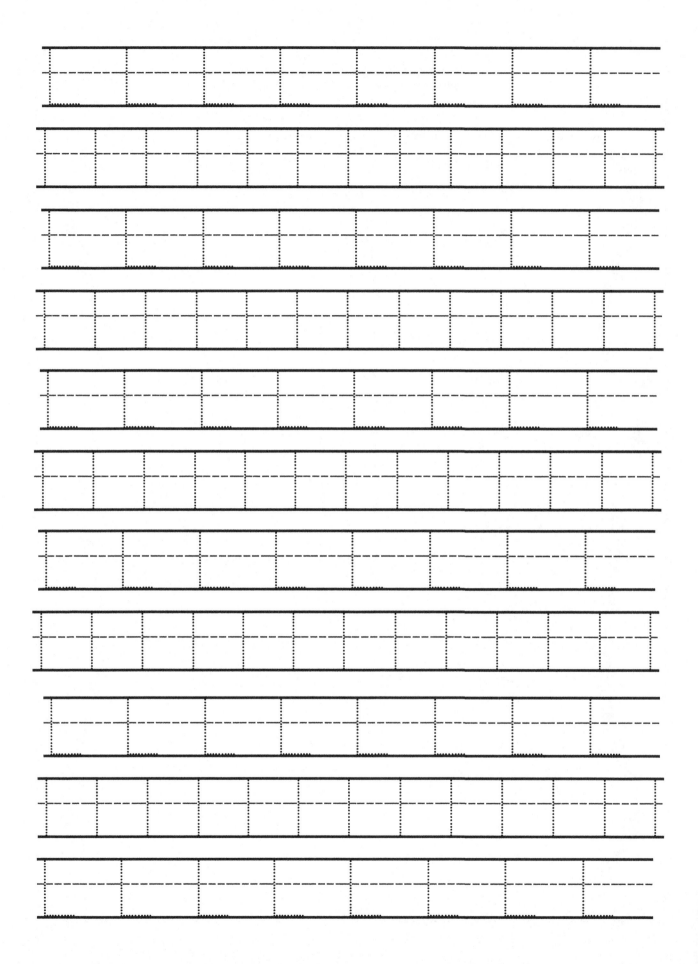

Letter Tracing
Upper Case

Trace the letter and color the picture.

Monkey

Trace the letter "M" and practice writing.

M M M M M M M M

Letter Tracing
Lower Case

Trace the letter and color the picture.

mask

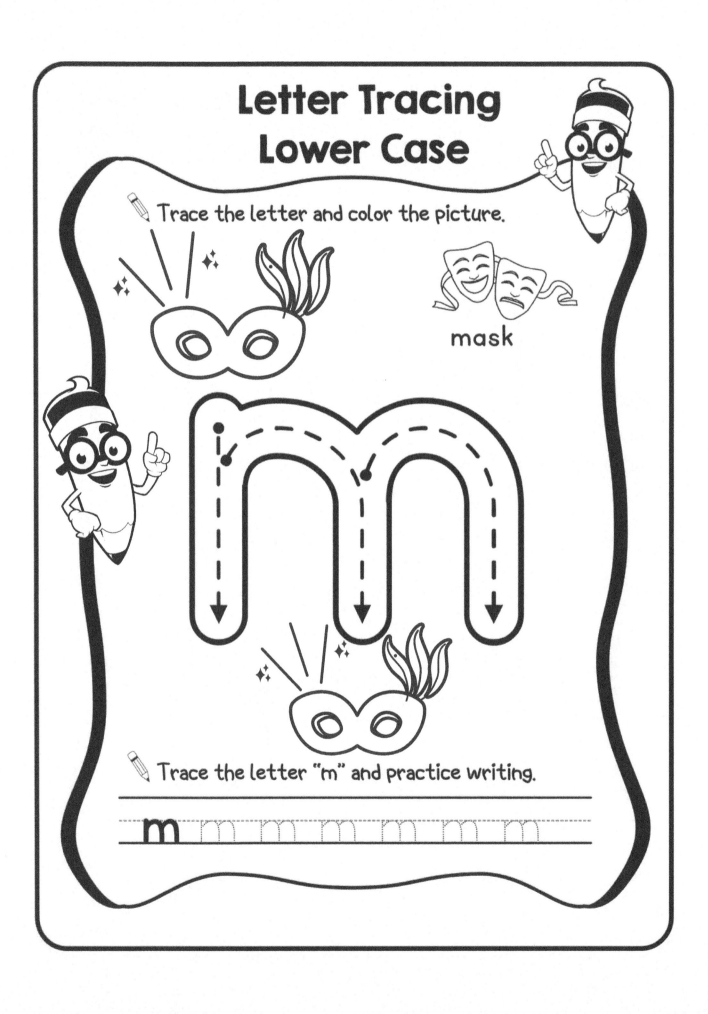

Trace the letter "m" and practice writing.

m m m m m m m m

Letter Tracing
Upper Case

Trace the letter and color the picture.

Noodles

Trace the letter "N" and practice writing.

Letter Tracing
Lower Case

Trace the letter and color the picture.

nest

Trace the letter "n" and practice writing.

n

Letter Tracing
Upper Case

Trace the letter and color the picture.

Octopus

O

Trace the letter "O" and practice writing.

Letter Tracing
Lower Case

Trace the letter and color the picture.

orange

Trace the letter "o" and practice writing.

Letter Tracing
Upper Case

Trace the letter and color the picture.

Pizza

Trace the letter "P" and practice writing.

P P P P P P P P P P P

Letter Tracing
Lower Case

✏️ Trace the letter and color the picture.

Panda

✏️ Trace the letter "p" and practice writing.

p p p p p p p p p

P P P P P P P P P

p p p p p p p p p

P P P P P P P P P

p p p p p p p p p

P P P P P P P P P

p p p p p p p p p

P P P P P P P P P

p p p p p p p p p

P P P P P P P P P

Letter Tracing
Upper Case

Trace the letter and color the picture.

Queen

Q

Trace the letter "Q" and practice writing.

Q Q Q Q Q Q Q Q

Letter Tracing
Lower Case

Trace the letter and color the picture.

queen

Trace the letter "q" and practice writing.

q q q q q q q q q q

Letter Tracing
Upper Case

Trace the letter and color the picture.

Rainbow

Trace the letter "R" and practice writing.

R R R R R R R R R R R R

Letter Tracing
Lower Case

✏️ Trace the letter and color the picture.

rocket

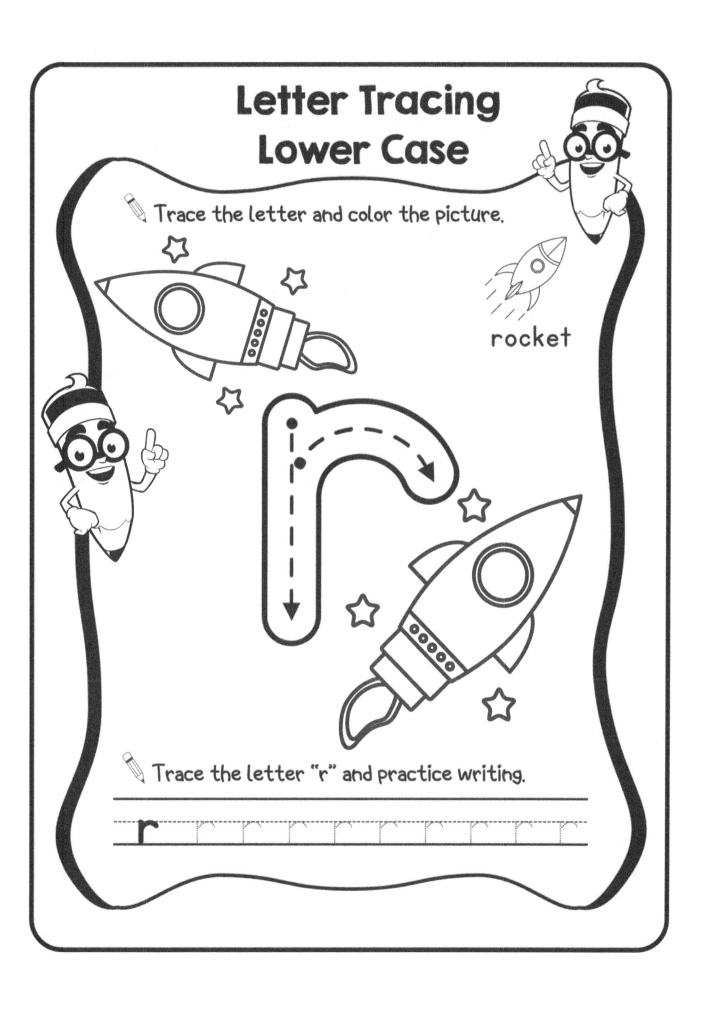

✏️ Trace the letter "r" and practice writing.

r

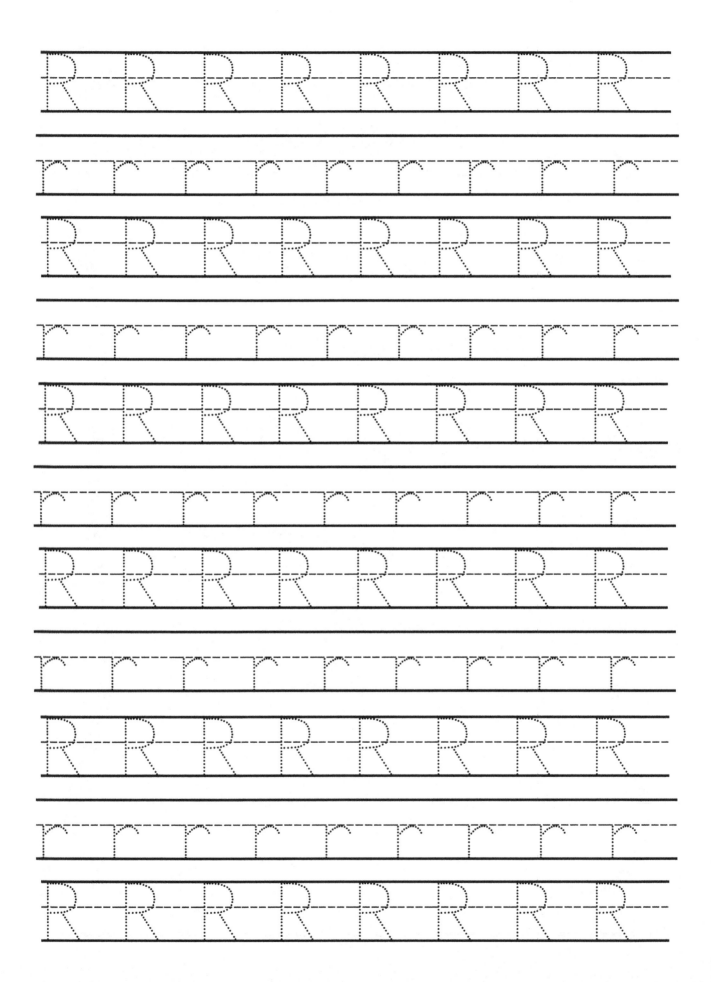

Letter Tracing
Upper Case

Trace the letter and color the picture.

Salad

Trace the letter "S" and practice writing.

S S S S S S S S S S

Letter Tracing
Lower Case

✏️ Trace the letter and color the picture.

strawberry

S

✏️ Trace the letter "s" and practice writing.

s s s s s s s s s s

Letter Tracing
Upper Case

Trace the letter and color the picture.

Tree

Trace the letter "T" and practice writing.

Letter Tracing
Lower Case

Trace the letter and color the picture.

tomato

Trace the letter "t" and practice writing.

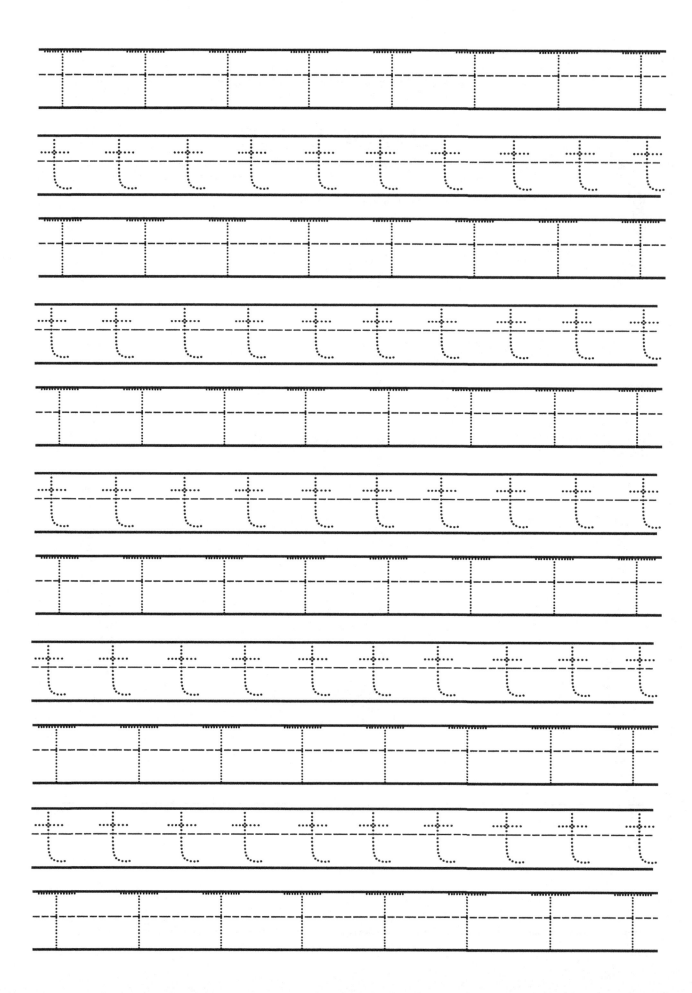

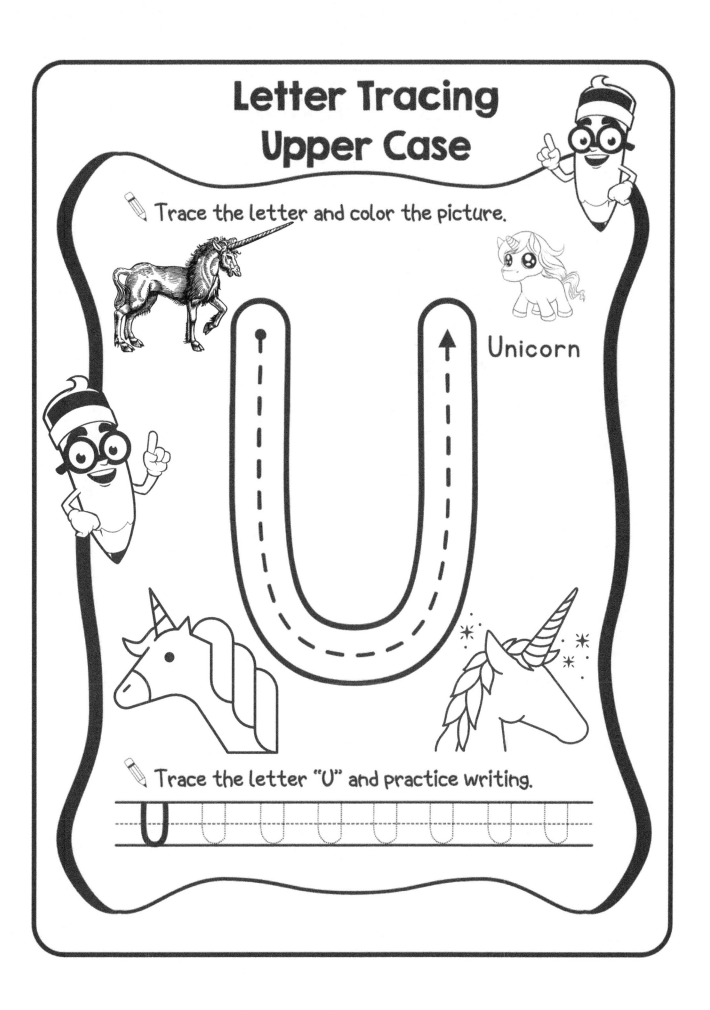

Letter Tracing
Upper Case

Trace the letter and color the picture.

Unicorn

Trace the letter "U" and practice writing.

Letter Tracing
Lower Case

Trace the letter and color the picture.

umbrella

Trace the letter "u" and practice writing.

u u u u u u u u u

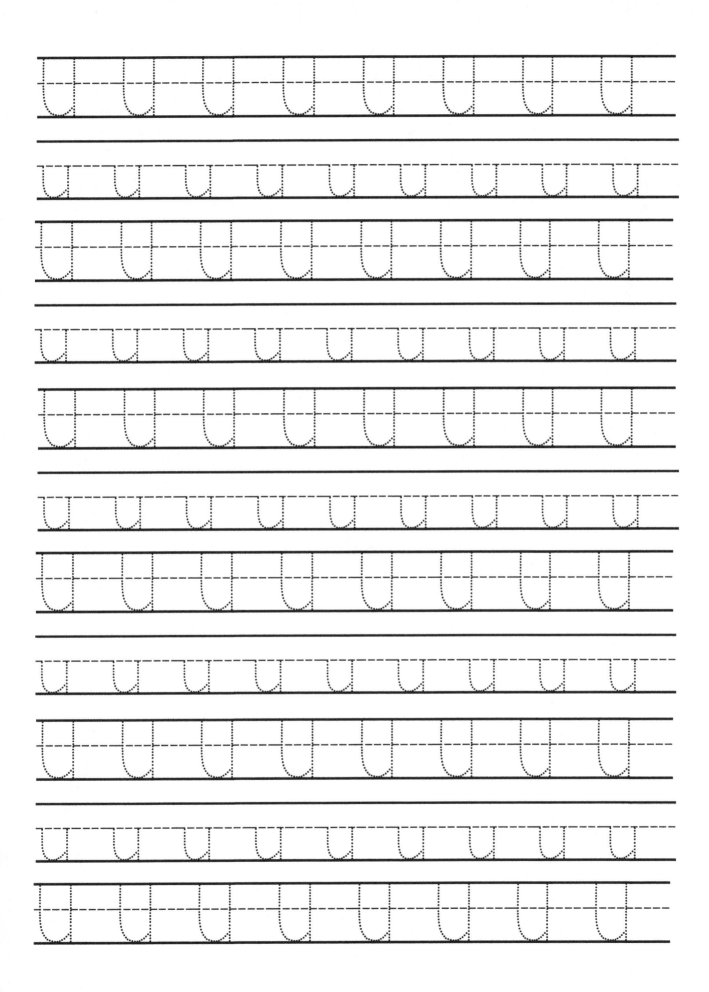

Letter Tracing
Upper Case

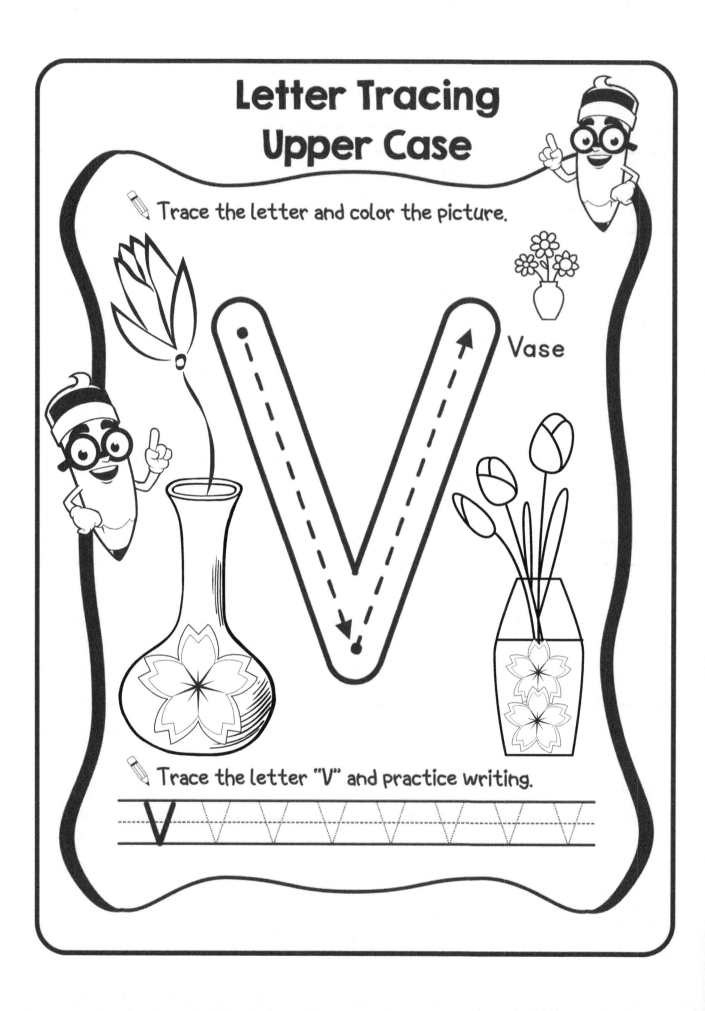

✏️ Trace the letter and color the picture.

Vase

✏️ Trace the letter "V" and practice writing.

Letter Tracing
Lower Case

Trace the letter and color the picture.

vulture

Trace the letter "v" and practice writing.

v v v v v v v v v v

Letter Tracing
Upper Case

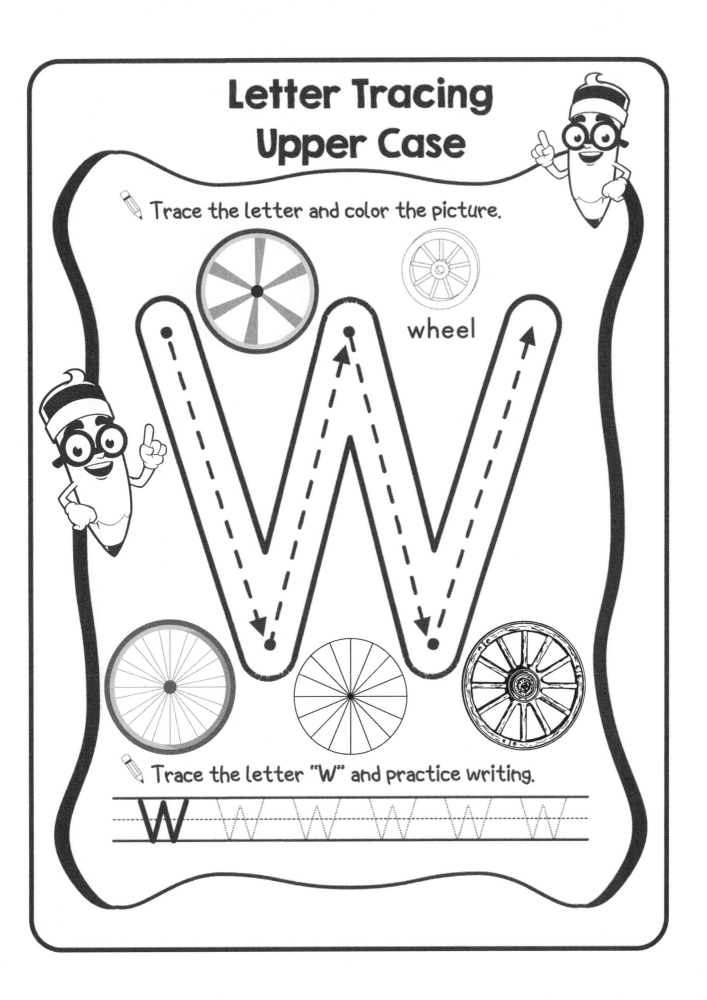

Trace the letter and color the picture.

wheel

Trace the letter "W" and practice writing.

Letter Tracing
Lower Case

Trace the letter and color the picture.

wand

Trace the letter "w" and practice writing.

Letter Tracing
Upper Case

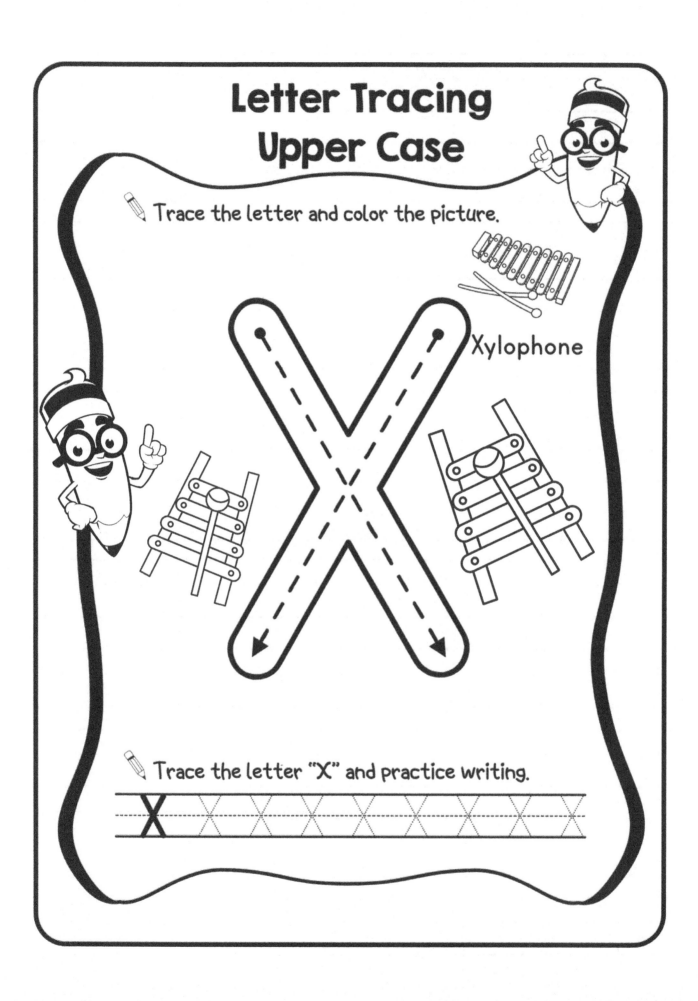

✏️ Trace the letter and color the picture.

Xylophone

✏️ Trace the letter "X" and practice writing.

Letter Tracing
Lower Case

✏️ Trace the letter and color the picture.

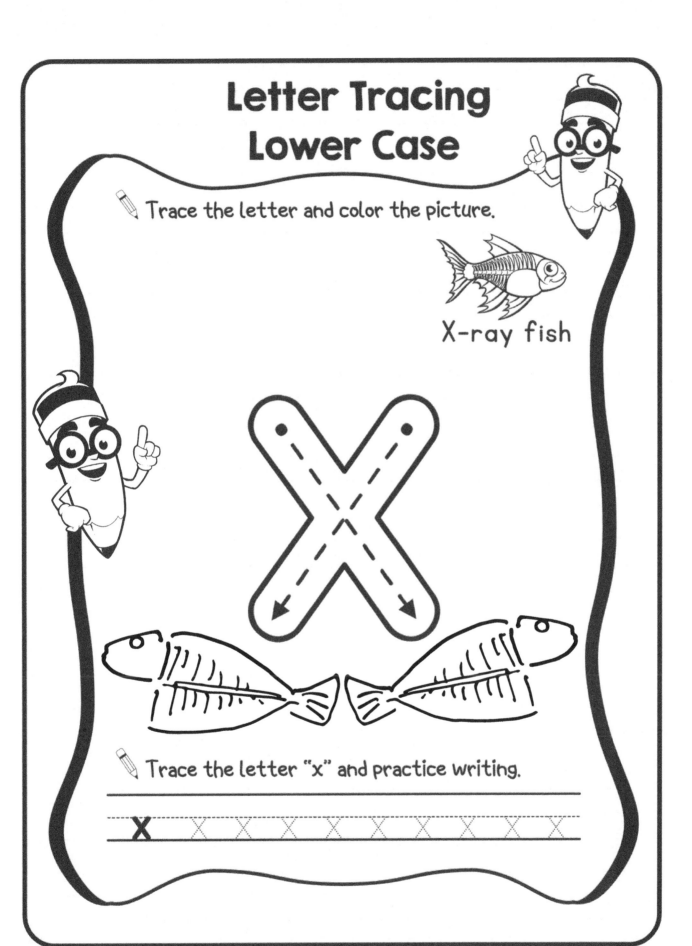

X-ray fish

✏️ Trace the letter "x" and practice writing.

x x x x x x x x x

Letter Tracing
Upper Case

✏️ Trace the letter and color the picture.

Yak

Y

✏️ Trace the letter "Y" and practice writing.

Y Y Y Y Y Y Y Y Y

Letter Tracing
Lower Case

Trace the letter and color the picture.

yacht

y

Trace the letter "y" and practice writing.

y y y y y y y y y y

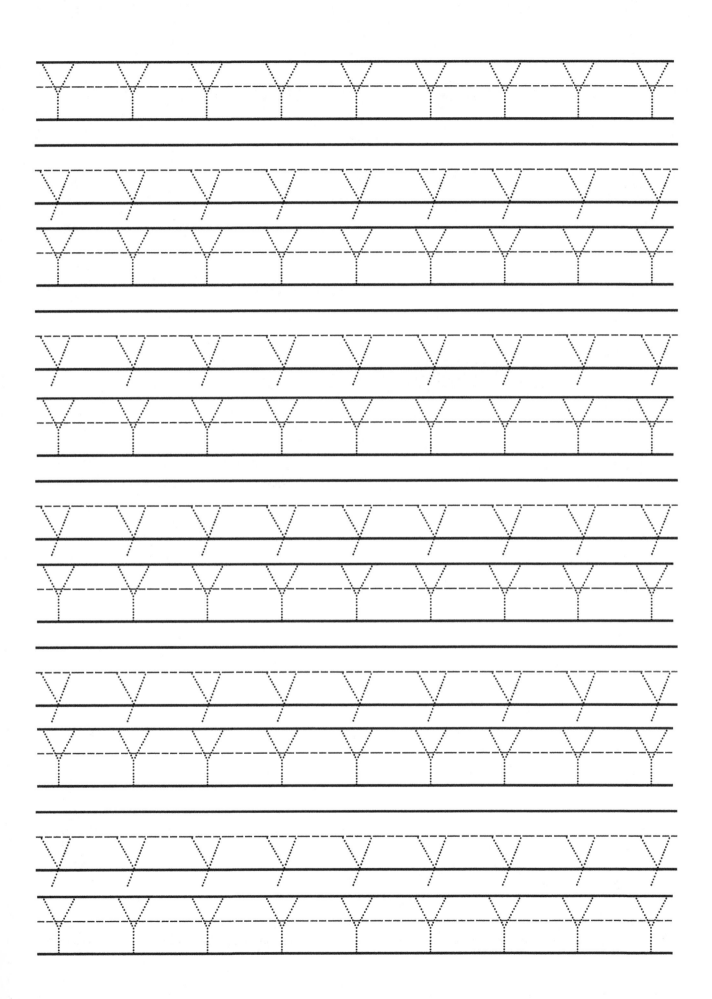

Letter Tracing
Upper Case

Trace the letter and color the picture.

Zebra

Trace the letter "Z" and practice writing.

Letter Tracing
Lower Case

Trace the letter and color the picture.

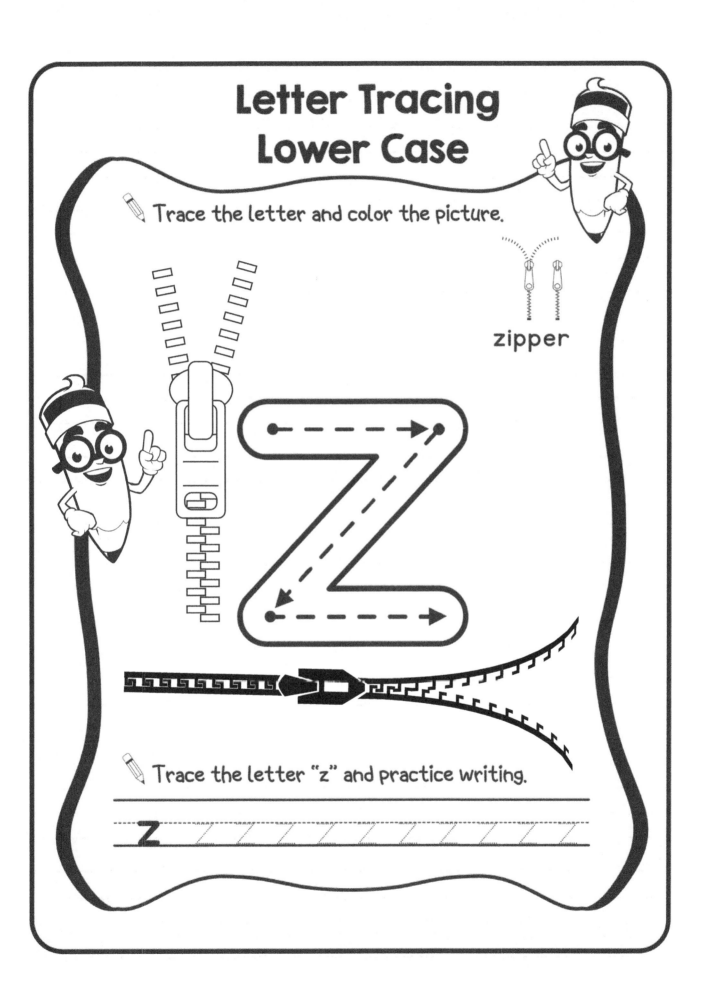

zipper

Trace the letter "z" and practice writing.

z

Number Tracing

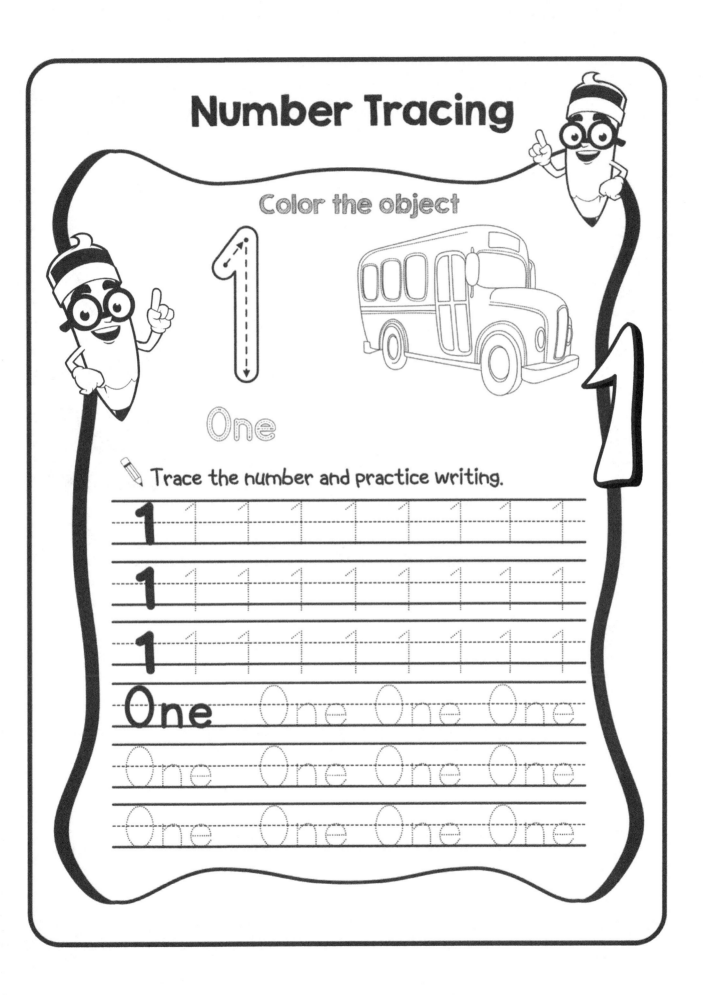

Color the object

1

One

✏ Trace the number and practice writing.

1 1 1 1 1 1 1 1 1 1

1 1 1 1 1 1 1 1 1 1

1 1 1 1 1 1 1 1 1 1

One One One One

One One One One

One One One One

Number Tracing

Color the object

2
Two

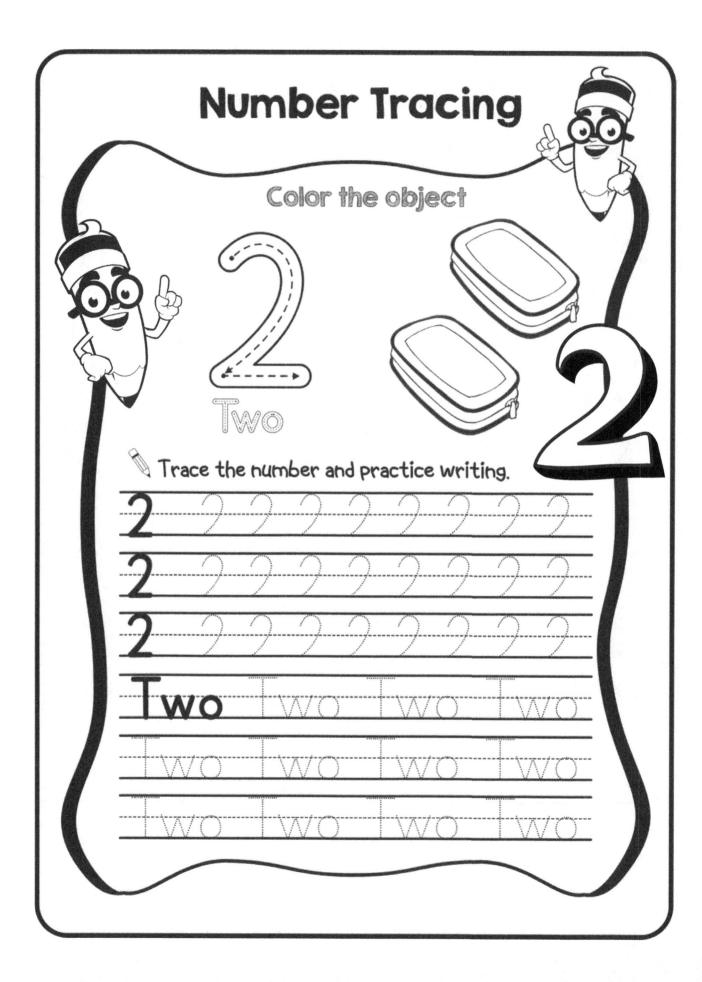

✏ Trace the number and practice writing.

2 2 2 2 2 2 2 2
2 2 2 2 2 2 2 2
2 2 2 2 2 2 2 2

Two Two Two Two
Two Two Two Two
Two Two Two Two

Number Tracing

Color the object

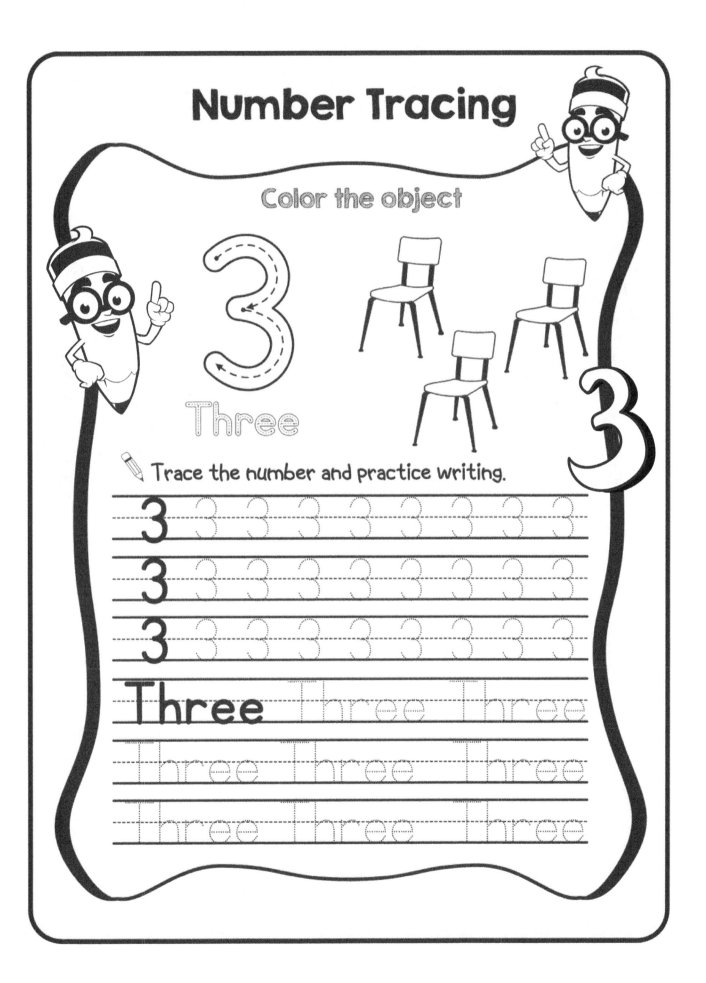

3

Three

✏ Trace the number and practice writing.

3 3 3 3 3 3 3 3
3 3 3 3 3 3 3 3
3 3 3 3 3 3 3 3

Three Three Three
Three Three Three
Three Three Three

Number Tracing

Color the object

4

Four

✏️ Trace the number and practice writing.

4
4
4

Four Four Four Four
Four Four Four Four
Four Four Four Four

Number Tracing

Color the object

5
Five

✏ Trace the number and practice writing.

5 5 5 5 5 5 5 5
5 5 5 5 5 5 5 5
5 5 5 5 5 5 5 5

Five Five Five Five
Five Five Five Five
Five Five Five Five

Number Tracing

Color the object

6

Six

✏️ Trace the number and practice writing.

6 6 6 6 6 6 6 6 6 6

6 6 6 6 6 6 6 6 6 6

6 6 6 6 6 6 6 6 6 6

Six Six Six Six Six

Six Six Six Six Six

Six Six Six Six Six

Number Tracing

Color the object

7

Seven

✏️ Trace the number and practice writing.

7 7 7 7 7 7 7 7 7 7

7 7 7 7 7 7 7 7 7 7

7 7 7 7 7 7 7 7 7 7

Seven Seven Seven

Seven Seven Seven

Seven Seven Seven

Number Tracing

Color the object

8

Eight

✏️ Trace the number and practice writing.

8
8
8

Eight Eight Eight
ight ight ight
ight Eight ight

Number Tracing

Color the object

9

Nine

✏️ Trace the number and practice writing.

9 9 9 9 9 9 9 9 9 9 9
9 9 9 9 9 9 9 9 9 9 9
9 9 9 9 9 9 9 9 9 9 9

Nine Nine Nine Nine
Nine Nine Nine Nine
Nine Nine Nine Nine

Number Tracing

Color the object

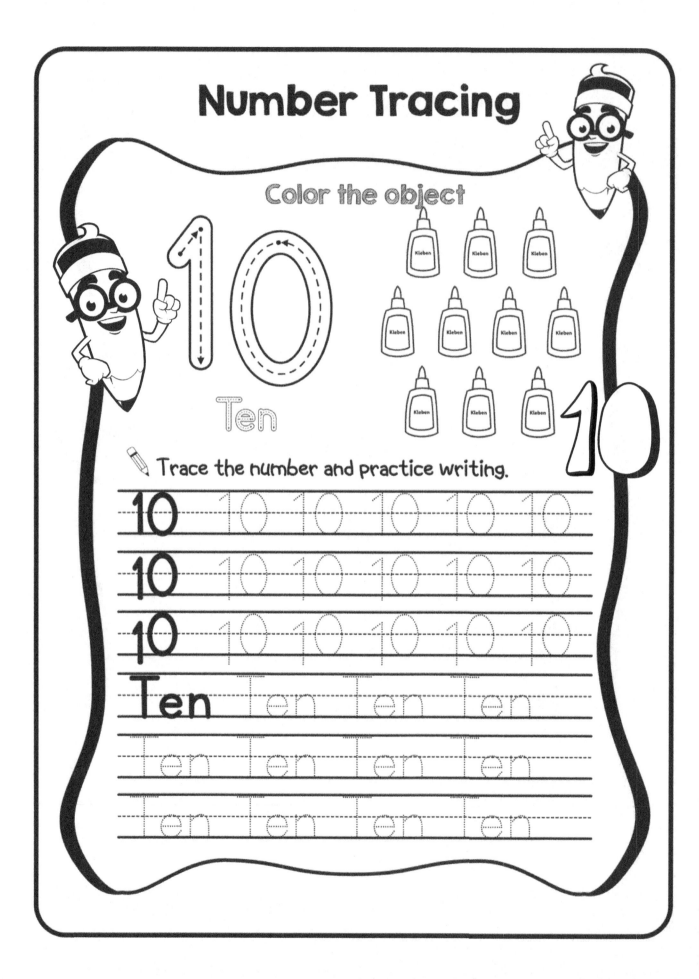

10

Ten

✏️ Trace the number and practice writing.

10 10 10 10 10 10

10 10 10 10 10 10

10 10 10 10 10 10

Ten Ten Ten Ten

Ten Ten Ten Ten

Ten Ten Ten Ten

CERTIFICATE OF COMPLETION

This certificate is presented to

for learning to write!

Date _____

Made in the USA
Monee, IL
26 May 2022

97027957R00057